ST. MARGARET'S RECIPE BOOK

St. Margaret's Recipe Book

ST. MARGARET'S CHURCH

St. Margaret's Church, Oxford

ST MARGARET'S RECIPE BOOK

FOOD FOR FAMILY AND FRIENDS

IN LOVING MEMORY OF MICHÈLE CRAWFORD
AND WITH THANKS TO EVE BARSHAM FOR THE IDEA!

OXFORD, JUNE 2024

ST MARGARET'S CHURCH, OXFORD OX2 6RX

Forward

REV'D CLAIRE BROWES

I wonder how you keep your recipes. Are they neatly written up in a book? Organised alphabetically in a folder? A set of bookmarks on your web browser? When my grandmother died, I inherited all of her recipes – she didn't keep them in a neat book but in bundles labelled 'starter', 'vegetables', etc. If I am honest, I have barely cooked a single one of them, but they feel too important to part with. We cook and eat every day and the recipes she had collected over a lifetime tell a story about who she was. There are cards cut from the side of flour boxes from the 1950s, cuttings from 80s magazines, many handwritten ones and some in handwriting which is not her own, recipes passed to her from other people. There are recipes from her own mother in there too. Recipes often have stories to tell and connect us with those we love.

This set of recipes reflects our community: some have a particularly special story or significance, others are just family favourite meals.

The cookbook is raising money for the Gatehouse Counselling Service.

From the Gatehouse website
https://oxfordgatehouse.org

The Gatehouse is an award-winning community drop-in centre with over 30 years' worth of experience of reaching out to, and supporting, adults who are homeless, vulnerably housed, on low or no income, and/or looking for company & community. We operate on an open access basis as our guests can face many barriers that lead to marginalisation and social isolation. As the years have gone by, we have found ever more ways of supporting guests in overcoming challenges. We do this by consulting, listening, and embedding co-production. We also involve guests (the users of our service) in decision making and developing our services to meet their needs.

Starters & Salads

-7-

Main Courses

-27-

Puddings

-57-

Biscuits & Cakes

-85-

STARTERS & SALADS

HOMEMADE FALAFELS

                                               LYNSEY BENNET

ST. MARGARET'S SOUP

                                               KATHRYN BUNCH

CAULIFLOWER SALAD

                                               THALIA CARR

COLD CHICKEN IN MANGO SAUCE

                                               MICHÈLE CRAWFORD

CASHEW BALLS IN MANGO SAUCE

                                               MICHÈLE CRAWFORD

SEARED SCALLOPS & PEA PUREE

                                               CAROL GOODALL

VEGAN SWEET POTATO & BROWN RICE SALAD

                                               SUSIE HARRIS

LENTIL, FETA, & TOMATO SALAD

                                             TALBOT-PONSONBY FAMILY

CHICKPEA & ROAST VEGETABLE SALAD

                                             TALBOT-PONSONBY FAMILY

STUFFED EGGS

                                             CARA THOMAS

HOMEMADE FALAFELS

Lynsey Bennet

I get 16-20 falafels from this recipe, which serves 4 as a main course if you prefer. You can add to this spice mix to your taste: harissa paste, fresh coriander, chilli flakes, sesame seeds, etc.

1 large onion
4 cloves garlic
1 tsp cumin seed
1 tsp smoked paprika
1 tsp ground coriander
1 tsp ground cumin
2 tins chickpeas
1 beaten egg
1-2 tbsp breadcrumbs/stuffing mix

1. Chop and fry the onion, garlic and spices for five to ten minutes until soft.
2. Drain the chickpeas and add to the pan. Fry for another ten minutes to dry the chickpeas out.
3. Mash the mixture and turn it into a bowl
4. Add the egg to bind
5. Add breadcrumbs to make it the consistency needed to form small patties/balls
6. Form 16 - 20 balls and shallow fry until brown
7. Serve with pita, hummus and salad

St Margaret's Soup Dragon

ST. MARGARET'S SOUP

Kathryn Bunch

This is very much a 'sort of' recipe so the vegetables could be varied depending on what was available or needed using and other types of stock could be substituted.
It freezes well so is a great winter standby.

1 large onion
1 clove garlic
250g carrots
200g tinned tomatoes
125g red lentils
1 vegetable stock cube, dissolved in 1 litre water
Salt and pepper

1. Peel and roughly chop the onion, top, tail and scrub carrots (or peel if necessary).
2. Heat vegetable oil in a large saucepan and fry onions, carrots and garlic until soft but without browning.
3. Add remaining ingredients and simmer until the vegetables and lentils are cooked (around 40 minutes).
4. Blitz the soup in a liquidiser or food processor and adjust the seasoning to taste.

CAULIFLOWER SALAD

Thalia Carr

1 Cauliflower
Oil
Salt
Pepper
2 tbsp Lemon juice
1 tbsp lemon zest
1 tsp Dijon mustard
¾ cup of grains – this could be rice, couscous, bulghur wheat or freekeh etc.
½ cup of raisins/ currants/ pomegranate seeds/ redcurrants/cranberries or similar
Veg stock cube
3 tbsp of finely chopped fresh mint or parsley

1. Heat oven to 220C.
2. Break the cauliflower into florets and coat in oil (olive oil is great if you have it).
3. Bake in the oven until browning (about 20 mins).
4. While it's cooking, cook your grain in the right amount of water (normally twice the quantity of the grain) and add the veg stock cube to that water.
5. While that is cooking, make a salad dressing with 4 tablespoons olive oil, the lemon juice, mustard, salt and pepper and lemon zest.
6. When everything is ready combine it all and adjust seasoning.
7. Eat cold – or hot if you can't wait, that's also nice.

Cold Chicken in Mango Sauce

COLD CHICKEN IN MANGO SAUCE

Michèle Crawford

The quantities here are approximate as I always make it by instinct and taste rather than by measurements. For a vegetarian version, see overleaf.

4 skinless chicken breasts
1 large or 2 smaller ripe mangoes (worth buying in advance to ensure ripeness)
Approx. "top end of a thumb" of fresh ginger
Carton of double cream
Bunch of fresh coriander

1. Preheat the oven to 200 C.
2. Season the chicken breasts and seal in a frying pan with a little butter.
3. Transfer to the oven to cook through, but try to avoid the outsides becoming too brown or hardened. When cooked, cool and cut into bite size chunks.
4. Cut open the mango(es) by slicing down the sides and then peeling round the central bit with the stone.
5. Put the flesh from around the stone and about half the rest of the flesh into a liquidizer or processor and puree.
6. Chop the rest of the mango into small bits, reserving a few of the prettier slices to garnish.
7. While the chicken is cooking, chop the ginger finely and cook for a couple of minutes in the frying pan in the buttery residue from browning the chicken.
8. Add the mango, stirring it all together, and most of the carton of cream, but check by tasting to make sure that the flavours of mango and ginger are not drowned. Taste to check the seasoning and allow it to bubble together for a few minutes.
9. Chop the leaves of the coriander, and a bit of stalk usually seems not to matter, and add to the sauce. It should be flecked with green, and all the flavours should be blended.
10. Cool, then mix with the chicken and Garnish with mango slices and coriander leaves.

CASHEW NUT BALLS IN MANGO SAUCE

Michèle Crawford

For a vegetarian version, the same sauce for the cold chicken goes very well with cashew nut balls.

Chopped cashew nuts
Breadcrumbs
Onions
Tomatoes
Herbs
Vegetarian stock thickened with a little flour

1. Preheat the oven.
2. Mixed the ingredients together.
3. Form into round dollops and then bake for about half an hour.

SEARED SCALLOPS & PEA PUREE

Carol Goodall

For the puree:
1 lb peas (thawed if frozen)
2 tbsp olive oil
Salt and pepper

For the scallops:
4 slices prosciutto
1 tbps olive oil
1 tbps butter
4 large or 8 small scallops, 1/2" thick
Salt and pepper
Extra virgin olive oil for drizzling
Pea shoots for garnish (optional)

1. Make the puree: Bring a saucepan of salted water to a rolling boil. Cook the peas until they're just tender, 3 to 4 minutes. Strain them in a colander, reserving about ½ cup of their cooking water. Put the peas in a blender with the olive oil, salt and pepper to taste, and a touch of the reserved cooking water, and blend until smooth.
2. Make the scallops: Preheat the oven to 350°F. Line a baking sheet with aluminium foil and lay the prosciutto on top. Lay a second sheet of foil on top of the prosciutto, and then set a second baking sheet on top. This will ensure that the prosciutto stays flat as it cooks. Bake for 10 to 15 minutes. Remove and set aside until needed.
3. In a sauté pan, heat the oil and butter over medium-high heat. Add the scallops and cook for 1 minute to 90 seconds on one side, then flip and cook for 30 seconds to 1 minute on the other, basting them frequently with the oil and butter and seasoning them with salt and pepper, until they are nicely browned and almost cooked through. Remember, they will keep cooking in their residual heat once you've set them aside.
4. Place 2 to 3 spoons of pea puree on each serving plate. Top it with the scallops, then crumble the crispy prosciutto over the top. Drizzle with a little extra virgin olive oil and garnish with the pea shoots, if desired.

Seared Scallops & Pea Puree

VEGAN SWEET POTATO & BROWN RICE SALAD

Susie Harris

This can be eaten warm or cold, as a main salad dish, or with extra protein added- cold chicken, tofu, a fried egg on top is also delicious! It is very versatile and excellent for a pot luck bring and share. It has appeared at church bring and share a few times and gone down well!!

1 sachet quick cook brown rice - I like basmati
1 sweet potato medium to large
1 can of sweetcorn (or equivalent from frozen)
1 can of black beans (or can use can of chickpeas or any other non sauce beans)
1/4 cucumber
1/2 red onion
1/2 tsp garlic powder
2 tsp butter
For the dressing:
3 tablespoons olive oil
1 Tablespoon balsamic vinegar
1 teaspoon Dijon or wholegrain mustard
1 tablespoon honey
Salt and pepper to taste

1. Bake whole sweet potato in oven or roast in air fryer for one hour.
2. Cook brown rice in microwave, 2 mins.
3. Drain beans and cook them in the microwave with a teaspoon of butter and garlic powder for 2.5 mins in microwave in a covered dish.
4. Empty into rice when hot then repeat this process with the sweetcorn until it is cooked- 3-4 minutes in microwave with a teaspoon of butter.
5. Make the dressing by mixing all the ingredients well and add into the hot ingredients and mix through the salad. Its important to do it at this stage to maximise flavours.
6. Chop cucumber into small pieces (quarter it and then slice) and add.
7. Chop red onion into small pieces and add.
8. De-skin then cut baked sweet potato into small pieces and add.
9. Mix together and serve.

LENTIL, FETA, & TOMATO SALAD

Talbot-Ponsonby Family

A staple of ours during the summer.
This makes enough for 4-6.

8oz dried puy lentils
24 fl oz veg. stock
1 packet cherry tomatoes – c.300g
1 packet feta cheese (c 200g)
4-5 spring onions
Olive oil
Vinegar (white wine and/or balsamic)

1. Rinse the lentils, bring them to the boil in the stock and simmer for about 20 minutes until tender.
2. Add a splash of white wine at the beginning for flavour if desired.
3. Meanwhile, halve the cherry tomatoes, finely chop the spring onions and dice the feta.
4. Mix all these with the cooked and drained lentils in a large bowl and dress with the olive oil and vinegar.
5. Serve with fresh sourdough or ciabatta, and a green salad.

CHICKPEA & ROAST VEGETABLE SALAD

Talbot-Ponsonby Family

Another summer staple – serves 4-6. We vary the veg that is roasted depending on what comes in the veg box but it is good to get a colourful mix. Rather than roast it, you could sauté or grill it if you prefer.

1 red onion

Some or all of:
A sweet pepper
1-2 courgettes
Butternut squash
A few cherry tomatoes (maybe 100g)

400g tin of chickpeas, drained and rinsed
1 packet Halloumi cheese (c.225g)
Thyme (fresh or dried)
Olive oil
Vinegar (white wine and/or balsamic)

1. Cut the onion into wedges and the other vegetables into bite-sized chunks, and halve the cherry tomatoes.
2. Mix with the thyme, toss in 1-2 tbsp olive oil and roast them all at 200o C for about 20 minutes until the courgette and squash are cooked.
3. Slice the halloumi fairly thin and then fry, preferably on a griddle pan so it gets stripy.
4. Mix the roasted vegetables, halloumi and chickpeas in a large bowl and dress with olive oil and vinegar.
5. Serve with fresh sourdough or ciabatta.

STUFFED EGGS

Cara Thomas

These are much loved by my children - they make
me make them for all our church pot-lucks!

12 eggs
120g crème fraiche
1 tbsp any roasted ground spice mix - I usually use a mix of coriander and cumin
1/2 tsp finely ground salt
Coriander or celery leaves, finely chopped
A pinch of paprika powder

1. Boil the eggs for 5 mins, drain and cover and then let them steam for 5 minutes.
2. Place the eggs in ice cold water and allow to cool - at least for an hour.
3. Shell the eggs as carefully as you can and gently dry the whites on some kitchen towel.
4. Halve the eggs and empty the yolks into a bowl. They should be cooked through but slightly soft.
5. Place the egg whites on a presentation plate, hole side up. You can slice a small sliver of the egg white at the bottom which will keep them from rolling.
6. Mash the yolks with a fork and combine thoroughly with the crème fraiche and spices to form the filling.
7. Divide the mixture into 24 in the bowl and spoon into the egg white halves.
8. Decorate with the leaves and dust with the paprika.

MAIN COURSES

VEGAN NUT ROAST — **FRANCES BAGNALL-OAKELEY**

BUTTERNUT SQUASH PIE — **LYNSEY BENNETT**

MAMIE'S RATATOUILLE — **CLAIRE BROWES**

CHICKEN WITH APRICOTS — **LIZ CARMICHAEL**

LAMB, PORT & CRANBERRY HOTPOT — **CAROL GOODALL**

SWEET & SOUR PORK — **BARBARA LEVICK**

PATSY'S GOAT'S CHEESE & SPINACH SOUFFLÉ — **MCSHANE FAMILY**

TURKEY MEATBALLS — **EMMA RONALD**

MEXICAN CHILLI CON CARNE — **ESTHER SELZER**

PASTA WITH RED STUFF — **HUGH SERIES**

CORONATION QUICHE — **HUGH SERIES**

THAI SALMON — **TALBOT-PONSONBY FAMILY**

CORIANDER SALMON — **CARA THOMAS**

CUMIN & CHICKEN RICE — **CARA THOMAS**

28 - ST. MARGARET'S CHURCH

VEGAN NUT ROAST

Frances Bagnall-Oakeley

This is my go-to vegan option for Christmas dinner - a BBC classic
and low-stress as it can be prepared ahead.
It's very dense so allow plenty of time for reheating!

300g/10½oz mixed nuts, almonds, hazelnuts, walnuts, etc
1 vegan-friendly vegetable stock cube
2 tbsp extra virgin olive oil, plus extra for greasing
1 onion, finely chopped
2 celery sticks, finely chopped
1 leek, trimmed and thinly sliced
2 carrots, coarsely grated
2 garlic cloves, crushed
4 tbsp cashew butter
180g/6oz cooked chestnuts, broken into small pieces
75g/2½oz dried cranberries
20g/¾oz bunch fresh parsley, finely chopped
1 lemon, finely grated zest only
4 tbsp milk alternative, such as soya or almond
1 tsp sea salt
freshly ground black pepper

1. Put the nuts and stock cube into a food processor and blitz on the pulse setting until chopped into small pieces, but not fully ground. If you don't have a food processor, chop all the nuts as finely as you can.
2. Preheat the oven to 200C/180C Fan/Gas 6. Lightly oil then line the base of a 900g/2lb loaf tin with baking paper.
3. Heat the oil in a large frying pan and gently fry the onion, celery, leek and carrots for 5 minutes, or until softened, stirring regularly. Add the garlic and cook for a few seconds more.
4. Tip into a mixing bowl and stir in the cashew nut butter. Add the chopped nuts, chestnuts, cranberries, parsley, lemon zest, soya or almond milk and salt. Season with lots of ground black pepper and stir until thoroughly mixed.

5. Spoon the mixture into the prepared loaf tin. Press down with a spoon firmly to compact the mixture.
6. Cover with foil and bake for 30 minutes. Remove the foil and bake for a further 20 minutes, or until the loaf is hot throughout and lightly browned.
7. Remove the tin carefully from the oven and cool for 5 minutes before loosening the edges of the loaf with a table knife and turning out onto a board or platter. Cut into thick slices and serve hot with vegan gravy.

Vegan Nut Roast

BUTTERNUT SQUASH PIE

Lynsey Bennet

You can make this with pumpkin or add red peppers, feta cheese or spinach to the filling

1 butternut squash
1 onion
4 cloves garlic
1 tsp smoked paprika
1 tsp cumin
1/2 tsp ground cinnamon
1 packet of puff pastry

1. Peel and slice the squash for roasting.
2. Add the diced onion, whole cloves of garlic and coat all with the spices.
3. Roast at 180C for 30 minutes.
4. Leave to cool.
5. Roll out the pastry.
6. Put the squash and add the squash so that it fills just half of this like this:

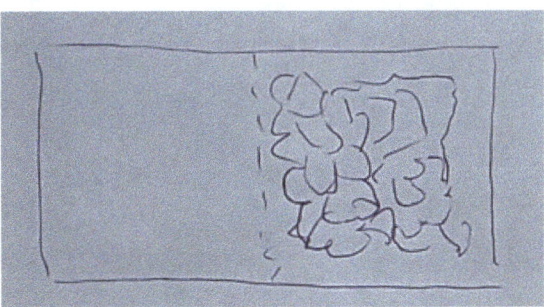

7. Fold the pastry over and crimp the edges.
8. Cook at 180C for 25 minutes until golden and crispy and eat hot or cold.

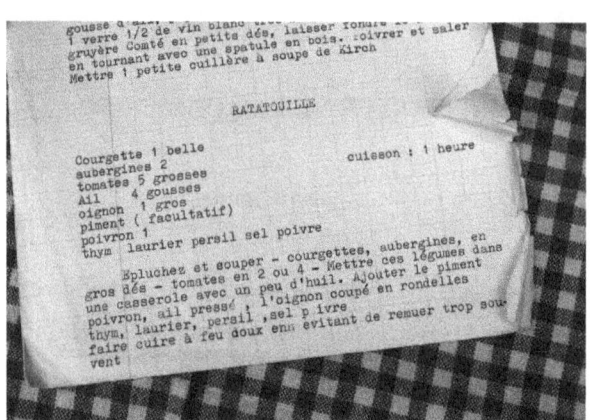

MAMIE'S RATATOUILLE

Claire Browes

From my Grandma's recipe collection, the original is written by typewriter on a paper with a number of other recipes. Makes enough for one family meal.
(I would add, to peel the tomatoes, it is much easier if they are boiled for 5 mins whole first with a scored cross on one end. The skin then just comes straight off.)

1 'good looking' courgette
2 aubergines
5 big tomatoes (peeled)
4 garlic cloves
1 big onion
Chili (optional)
1 pepper
Thyme, Bay & Parsley
Salt & Pepper

1. Peel and cut the courgettes and aubergines into large cubes, cut the tomatoes into fours.
2. Add these vegetables into a casserole dish or large saucepan with a little olive oil.
3. Add the chili, pepper, crushed garlic, onion (cut into circles), the herbs, salt and pepper.
4. Cook it all on a low heat trying to avoid stirring it too often for 1 hour.

CHICKEN WITH APRICOTS

Liz Carmichael

This is a tasty one, learnt decades ago from a student in Johannesburg who was receiving instructions from his sister by phone while he was cooking, so there are no precise amounts! Enjoy!

Enough uncooked chicken pieces for the number of diners, plus enough for seconds!
(Thighs and drumsticks are good, or a whole chicken cut into pieces)
Butter for frying
Dried herbs: oregano, basil, mixed herbs.
Salt and black pepper
Canned Cream of Tomato Soup; about 3-4 cans for a whole chicken)
Dried apricots (3 or 4 per person) halved.

1. Heat a non-stick frying pan or wok or a non-stick stew pan or casserole, and fry the chicken in butter with generous amounts of herbs, seasoning with salt & pepper, until skin is browned and meat partially cooked. If necessary transfer the chicken from the frying pan into a larger pan or casserole, etc.
2. Add tomato soup to cover the chicken well. Add the apricot pieces, and a little hot water from rinsing the cans. Bring to a simmer and cook for at least 30-45 minutes on the hob (stirring occasionally), or longer in the oven, until the chicken is well cooked.
3. Serve with rice or couscous and a salad or ratatouille.

Lamb, Port & Cranberry Hotpot

LAMB, PORT & CRANBERRY HOTPOT

Carol Goodall

1 tablespoon sunflower oil
6 lamb chump chops, about 750 g (1½ lb), halved
1 onion, chopped
125 g (4 oz) button mushrooms, sliced
2 tablespoons plain flour
450 ml (¾ pint) lamb stock
125 ml (4 fl. oz) ruby port
1 tablespoon tomato purée
1 tablespoon cranberry sauce
25 g (1 oz) dried cranberries (optional)
700 g (1 lb 7 oz) baking potatoes, thinly sliced
salt and pepper
chopped parsley, to garnish (optional)

1. Preheat the slow cooker if necessary – see manufacturer's instructions.
2. Heat the oil in a large frying pan, add the lamb and fry over a high heat until browned on both sides.
3. Lift out with a slotted spoon and transfer to a plate.
4. Add the onion to the pan and fry, stirring, for 5 minutes or until lightly browned. Add the mushrooms and cook for 2 minutes.
5. Stir in the flour, then gradually mix in the stock and port.
6. Add the tomato purée, cranberry sauce and dried cranberries, if using, and season to taste with salt and pepper. Bring to the boil, stirring.
7. Put the pieces of lamb in the base of the slow cooker pot, pour over the hot sauce and arrange the sliced potatoes on top, overlapping the slices in two layers.
8. Gently press the potatoes down into the sauce, cover and cook on high for 7–8 hours or until the lamb and potatoes are tender.
9. Sprinkle with parsley, if liked, and spoon into bowls.

SWEET & SOUR PORK

Barbara Levick

2 tbs oil
1 onion
750g pork in chunks (fat pork, such as belly, or lean pork are equally good)
2 tbs corn flour
300 ml stock
1 green pepper
1 tin of apricot halves, drained.
5 tbs of liquor from the tin
50 g sultanas
1 tbs honey
5 tbs wine vinegar
salt
1/2 tsp powdered ginger
To serve: rice or noodles, green salad

1. First brown the pork, put to one side, and soften the chopped onion in oil.
2. Stir in the corn flour, gradually adding the stock, stirring to make a thick sauce.
3. Cut the pepper into strips and add to the sauce with the apricots roughly chopped.
4. Add the apricot liquor, sultanas, honey, vinegar, salt and ginger and the browned meat.
5. Cook very gently for about 40 minutes and serve with rice or noodles and green salad.

PATSY'S GOAT'S CHEESE & SPINACH SOUFFLÉ

McShane Family

Note: the goat's cheese can be replaced with Cheddar (stronger = better), Stilton or any other cheese

30g butter
30g plain flour
150ml milk
4 medium / 3 large eggs
100g goat's cheese
100g spinach

1. Preheat oven to 180C.
2. Melt the butter in a small saucepan, add the flour and stir to make a roux. Gradually add the milk, stirring continuously until you have a thick, smooth sauce. Remove from the heat and allow to cool a little.
3. Separate the eggs into white and yolk – being very careful not to get any yolk into the white as otherwise the souffle will not rise.
4. Whisk the yolks and add to the sauce.
5. Cube the goat's cheese, cook the spinach, and add both to the sauce and season to taste with salt and black pepper.
6. Whisk the egg whites until firm (do this step last).
7. Take a spoonful of the whisked egg white and fold with a metal spoon into the sauce.
8. Then add the sauce to the rest of the whisked egg white and fold carefully in – doing this reasonably briskly.
9. Immediately put the mixture into a buttered soufflé dish (or individual ones) and put in the oven on the middle shelf for ~ 30 mins until set. Remove and serve immediately.

42 - ST. MARGARET'S CHURCH

TURKEY MEATBALLS

Emma Ronald

These turkey meatballs are a great favourite and make a delicious family meal. Serve with rice. You could also make these using chicken. Makes 24 meatballs (8 small portions or 4 adult portions). Suitable for freezing.

For the meatballs:
1 tsp olive oil
1 onion, peeled and chopped
150g (5oz) carrot, finely grated
500g (1 lb 2 oz minced turkey)
75g (3 oz) fresh breadcrumbs
75g (3 oz) crushed pineapple, drained
2 tsp soy sauce
1 tsp brown sugar
Salt and pepper (for babies over 12 months)
Flour
Vegetable oil, for frying

For the sauce:
1 onion, peeled and finely chopped
1 tbsp vegetable oil
1 x 400g (14oz) can chopped tomatoes
100 ml (3.5 fl oz) pineapple juice
1 tbsp soy sauce
1 tbsp dark brown sugar
Juice of half a lemon
Salt and pepper (for babies over 12 months)

1. Heat the oil in a small saucepan, add the onion and carrots, and sauté for 3 minutes until softened.
2. Remove from the pan and leave to cool.

3. Once cold, mix with the turkey mince, pineapple, soy sauce, sugar and seasoning (if using).
4. Transfer to a food processor and blend for a second or two.
5. Shape into about 24 balls using floured hands.
6. Heat the oil in a frying pan, add the turkey balls and sauté for a couple of minutes over a high heat to seal.
7. Then reduce the heat and cook for 6-8 minutes or until cooked through.
8. For the sauce, heat the oil in a small saucepan, add the onion and sauté for 5 minutes.
9. Stir in the remaining ingredients and simmer, uncovered, for 10 minutes.
10. Pour the sauce over the turkey balls and serve.

MEXICAN CHILLI CON CARNE

Esther Selzer

Serves 10. This recipe can easily be multiplied and freezes well.

5 tablespoons vegetable oil
2 large onions, chopped
1 chilli pepper, chopped
5 cloves garlic, chopped
2lb lean ground beef
3 (14.5oz) cans whole peeled tomatoes with liquid, chopped
1 ½ teaspoons salt
1 teaspoon freshly ground black pepper
1 ½ teaspoons ground cumin
½ tablespoon chilli powder
2 tablespoons paprika
2 tablespoons dried oregano
2 cinnamon sticks
6 whole cloves
2 (15.25 oz) cans red kidney beans, rinsed and drained

1. In a medium-sized stock pot, heat the oil over a medium heat. Sauté the onion, chilli pepper, and garlic, until soft.
2. Add the ground beef: cook and stir until the meat is browned.
3. Pour in the tomatoes with the liquid, salt, pepper, cumin, chilli powder, paprika, oregano, cinnamon sticks, and cloves. Cover and simmer for 45 minutes.
4. Stir in the kidney beans, and cook for another 15 minutes.
5. Remove cinnamon sticks.
6. Serve with plain white rice and sour cream.

Mexican Chilli Con Carne

PASTA WITH RED STUFF

Hugh Series

Serves 3-4. Just the thing for a quickly assembled dinner after choir practice on Friday evening.

Dried fusilli pasta (or any other shape you like) 80-100g per person
1 can chopped tomatoes
150 g mozzarella (the harder sort which isn't sold in water works better)
125g grated parmesan
Fresh basil, roughly torn up

1. Put tomatoes in a non-stick pan.
2. When hot, add parmesan first, and when it starts to melt into the tomatoes add the mozzarella.
3. While that's cooking, cook the pasta in boiling salted water (about 8-10 mins, or as per the packet instructions).
4. Add the basil to the sauce.
5. Mix the strained pasta into the tomato sauce and serve.

Coronation Quiche

CORONATION QUICHE

Hugh Series

The official recipe as served at St Margaret's
on the day of King Charles's coronation

For the pastry case:
250g plain flour, plus a little for dusting
50g cold butter, diced
50g lard (or use butter if you prefer)
4 tbsp milk, plus a splash
> or 250g block of ready-made shortcrust pastry

For the filling:
125ml milk
175ml double cream
2 medium eggs
1 tbsp chopped fresh tarragon
100g cheddar, grated
180g cooked spinach, liquid squeezed out and lightly chopped
> **60g cooked broad beans or soya beans (double pod the broad beans, if you like)**

You will need a 20cm loose-bottomed tart tin or a 20cm pastry ring

1. Sieve the flour into a bowl with ½ tsp salt. Add the butter and lard, and rub the mixture together using your fingertips until you get a sandy, breadcrumb-like texture.
2. Add the milk a little at a time and, using a cutlery knife, start to bring the dough together, using your hands, making sure it has no dry patches and feels smooth. Cover and allow to rest in the fridge for 30-45 mins.
3. Put a 20cm loose-bottomed tart tin or a 20cm pastry ring on a baking sheet.
4. Lightly flour the work surface and roll out the pastry to a circle a little larger than the top of the tin and approximately 5mm thick. Carefully lift the pastry into the tin and gently press into the corners, taking care not to have any holes or the mixture could leak. Cover and rest for a further 30 mins in the fridge.

5. Heat oven to 190C/170C fan. Line the pastry case with greaseproof paper – to do this cut a disc of greaseproof paper larger than the tin, scrunch it into a ball (this makes it more pliable), then unwrap and place it in the pastry case. Fill with baking beans or uncooked rice and bake blind for 20-25 until nicely golden and dry.
6. Carefully remove the greaseproof paper and baking beans, and return to the oven for 5 mins to dry.
7. Reduce the oven temperature to 160C/140C fan
8. Beat the milk, cream, eggs and herbs with some seasoning.
9. Scatter half of the grated cheese in the blind-baked base, top with the chopped spinach and beans, then pour over the liquid mixture. If required, gently give the mixture a delicate stir to ensure the filling is evenly dispersed, but be careful not to damage the pastry case.
10. Sprinkle over the remaining cheese.
11. Place into the oven and bake for 20-30 mins until set and very lightly golden.

THAI SALMON

Talbot-Ponsonby Family

This is based on a BBC Good Food recipe that seems to have disappeared from the website years ago. We printed it out about 12 years ago and have adapted it to make it simpler. We have found that the children have found the marinaded salmon a bit strong, so we often marinade 2 pieces (for the adults) and then cook all the salmon together in the sauce, remembering which were the unmarinated ones for the children. We don't always include coriander if not available.

The BBC recommends grilling or barbecuing the salmon but as we have an AGA, we usually roast it. This also allows the marinade to be poured over it before cooking, which helps.

4 salmon fillets (preferably skin off)
1 thumb sized red chilli, de-seeded and finely chopped (we often use only ½)
2 garlic cloves, finely chopped
1 tbsp fish sauce
1 tbsp sesame oil
2 tbsp runny honey
½ cucumber, diced
Coriander, handful, roughly chopped (if available)
4 tbsp sweet chilli sauce
Lime juice

1. Mix together the chilli, garlic, coriander (if available), fish sauce, sesame oil and honey in a bowl. 2. Put the salmon in and marinade in the fridge for anything from 20 minutes to overnight: the longer it marinades, the more strongly the salmon will be flavoured.
2. Put the salmon in a roasting tin and pour over the remainder of the marinade. Cover with silver foil and roast at 200º C for about 20 minutes. You may want to give it a further 5 minutes with the cover off so it goes a bit crisp at the edges.
3. Dice the cucumber and mix with the chilli sauce and a drop of lime juice
4. Serve the salmon with the cucumber / chilli sauce mix; we usually eat this this with rice and a green vegetable.

CORIANDER SALMON

Cara Thomas

This was one of the first recipes I devised for i-Spice, a book I wrote during the Covid lockdowns. It is good hot as a light summer curry with buttery rice or it can be served cold as part of a buffet or church pot-luck.

1 tbsp coriander seed
1 small onion
1 small piece of ginger
2 cloves garlic
2 large chillies
4 tbsp yoghurt
4 salmon fillets/steaks/tail cuts
Coriander leaf, chopped, for garnish
Lemon zest for garnish

1. Toast the coriander seeds in a dry pan until fragrant and then crush to a relatively fine powder in a pestle and mortar, although keep a little 'crunch'.
2. Process the ginger, garlic, onion and 1 chilli to a paste with 1 tbsp of yoghurt and half the coriander seed.
3. In a large bowl, mix the other half of the coriander seed, the paste and the yoghurt. Put the salmon in the same bowl and cover with the marinade and leave for an hour.
4. Preheat the oven to 225C.
5. Shake off the excess marinade on the salmon and then place the pieces on a lined baking sheet.
6. Roast for 10 minutes until the edges are charred. The salmon should be just slightly underdone and coral-pink inside.
7. Place in a hot serving dish.
8. Finely slice the remaining chilli and garnish with the chilli, coriander leaves and lemon zest before serving with rice.
9. Alternatively, after 6. allow to cool, garnish and serve alongside cold crisp lettuce leaves as part of a buffet or picnic.

CUMIN & CHICKEN RICE

Cara Thomas

Another recipe from my book - this is an easy weekday family dinner, as it is an all-in-one dish. Serve with yoghurt and mango chutney on the side.

2 tbsp cumin seed/1 heaped tbsp ground cumin
1/2 tsp salt
1 onion
4 cloves garlic
1 green chilli
100 ml coconut cream
200g long grain rice
400 ml water
4-8 chicken pieces (skin-on and bone-in)
75g (frozen) garden peas
Coriander leaf, chopped for garnish
Celery leaf, finely chopped for garnish
Spring onion, finely chopped for garnish

1. Preheat the oven to 200C.
2. Toast the cumin seeds if using in a dry pan, then lightly crush.
3. Process the salt, garlic, onion and the chilli to a fine paste with the coconut cream plus a cup of water and the cumin.
4. Use the paste to coat the chicken, with a little pushed under the skin.
5. Place the rice in a large oven dish and place the chicken and the marinade on top of the rice.
6. Pour 400ml of water over the rice and chicken and cover the dish tightly with tin foil. Bake for 30 mins covered.
7. Stir in the peas under the chicken, tossing the rice to ensure it doesn't stick to the bottom of the dish.
8. Roast uncovered for a further 15 mins to brown the skin of the chicken and garnish before serving.

PUDDINGS

TIRAMISU — LUCIA COSTANZO

NO-CHURN ICE CREAM — LUCIA COSTANZO

WHITE CHOCOLATE & COINTREAU ICE CREAM — MICHÈLE CRAWFORD

QUICK AND HEALTHY PANCAKES FOR ONE — SUSIE HARRIS

FRUIT BOMBE — BARBARA LEVICK

BAKED CHOCOLATE PUDDING — LUCIA NIXON

CHOCOLATE RASPBERRY CAKE — SAM SCHAD

GALETTE DES ROIS AU CHOCOLAT — SAM SCHAD

SCOTTISH TRIFLE — SAM SCHAD

LANY SELZER'S CHEESECAKE — SELZER FAMILY

TARTE TATIN — HUGH SERIES

CHOCOLATE FUDGE PUDDING — TALBOT-PONSONBY FAMILY

ROSE & CARDAMOM BLANCMANGE — CARA THOMAS

TIRAMISU

Lucia Costanzo

This delicious Italian dessert is incredibly easy to make and is absolutely delicious. It's actually a relatively new dessert and was probably invented in the 1970s in the Veneto area of Italy. There is no definitive recipe. Some modern Italian versions omit eggs and use condensed milk for example.

I have tried and tweaked many variations and this one is the best.

4 tablespoons of Tia Maria
2 tablespoons brandy
100 ml cold, strong black coffee, ideally espresso or made in a moka pot
16 to 18 sponge fingers/savoiardi biscuits
(depending on the size of the dish)
500g mascarpone cheese
2 medium eggs separated
4 tablespoons icing sugar
1 tablespoon of cocoa

1. Mix the brandy and Tia Maria with the coffee.
2. Dip sponge fingers in this mixture and lay in a shallow dish, about 20cm square.
3. Drizzle over a little more of the coffee mixture, but not so much that the sponge becomes soggy.
4. Separate the eggs.
5. Beat together the egg yolks and add the mascarpone, and icing sugar.
6. Whisk egg whites until stiff, but not dry, and fold into the mascarpone mixture.
7. Spoon half of the mixture over the sponge fingers.
8. Repeat this with another layer of soaked sponge fingers, and smooth over the rest of the mascarpone mixture.
9. Using a tea strainer, sieve cocoa powder over the top.
10. Let the tiramisu rest in the fridge for a few hours, or ideally overnight.

NO-CHURN ICE CREAM

Lucia Costanzo

No churn ice cream is incredibly easy to make and is absolutely delicious - if quite rich. I find that whipping cream (with a lower fat content than double cream) gives a better result. The alcohol is necessary in this recipe to stop the ice cream from freezing too hard. You can use all sorts of alcohol in this; vodka doesn't give any taste at all, but you could use brandy, rum, limoncello, Cointreau - or anything which has a reasonable alcohol content. They're all delicious.

This will keep fresh for a couple of weeks in the freezer.

397g tin of condensed milk
2 tablespoons of alcohol: see below
1 teaspoon vanilla bean extract, or a good-quality extract
1/4 of a teaspoon of fine salt
A 600ml tub of whipping cream (or double cream if you can't find this, see above)

1. Whisk together the condensed milk, alcohol, vanilla, and salt.
2. Separately, beat the cream until stiff peaks then add the boozy milk mixture.
3. Spoon into a freeze-able container and freeze for 6 to 8 hours.

WHITE CHOCOLATE & COINTREAU ICE CREAM

Michèle Crawford

This is a very useful recipe as you do not need an ice-cream maker, nor to keep stirring it while it freezes. I make it in a ring mould and fill the centre with strawberries or other berries. It could also be frozen in a loaf tin or even a bowl. It slices easily and makes about 8 portions

175g white chocolate, roughly chopped
2 egg yolks
50g caster sugar
284ml single cream
284ml double cream
Cointreau to taste (Grand Marnier or Armagnac also work well)

1. With an electric beater, whisk the egg yolks and sugar together until pale and smooth.
2. In a Pyrex bowl over a pan of simmering water, melt the white chocolate with the single cream. Don't let the water touch the bottom of the bowl.
3. When melted and smooth, pour over the egg and sugar mixture, whisking to mix thoroughly, then pour it all back into the bowl over simmering water.
4. Continue to heat gently until slightly thickened. Leave to cool.
5. Add Cointreau to taste when cool.
6. Whip the double cream and fold into the chocolate mixture. Give it another quick whisk at this stage to make sure that it is all amalgamated smoothly.
7. Pour into container and freeze. Don't take out of the freezer too long before serving. It slices easily with a knife dipped in hot water.
8. Serve with fresh berries.

Pancakes

Pancakes with toppings

QUICK AND HEALTHY PANCAKES FOR ONE

Susie Harris

Suggested toppings: blueberries and yogurt.
Optional Extras: 1 tsp cinnamon, 1 tsp vanilla extract. Honey, if banana is not ripe.

1 ripe banana
1 large egg
2 tbsp of flour- buckwheat works well, but could also use wholewheat.
1 tbsp olive oil for cooking.

1. Beat the egg.
2. Mash the banana and add them together.
3. Add in the flour and any flavourings.
4. Mix together but not too much.
5. Heat the pan with the olive oil.
6. When the pan is hot, (test by dropping a tiny bit of water and see if it hisses!) put half the mixture in, wait until it bubbles and turn!
7. Repeat.

FRUIT BOMBE

Barbara Levick

8 meringue nests
300ml whipping cream
Fruit puree and nuts, e.g. pureed plums and chopped macadamia nuts
Mint leaves to garnish

1. Line a pudding basin or similar with clingfilm.
2. Whip the cream to stiffness and fold in the meringues broken into large pieces.
3. Pack into the basin, cover with more clingfilm and seal with a lid or a rubber band.
4. Place in freezer, preferably overnight.
5. Half an hour before eating remove from the freezer, unwrap, and place in a dish.
6. Just before eating tip fruit puree over your bombe and decorate with mint leaves or nuts as appropriate. A good one is pureed plums with chopped macadamia nuts.

BAKED CHOCOLATE PUDDING

Lucia Nixon

Serves 4(-ish). It is incredibly good! The recipe came from my lovely sister-in-law Mary. You'll notice that I haven't said how many people it serves — that's because in our family of four we were lucky to get four good servings plus much smaller ones for seconds!

The only disadvantage to making this pudding is that you have to finish the preparation and baking between courses — but no one has ever complained about the result!

200g dark chocolate
200g butter
4 eggs
2 dl or 3/4 cup sugar
2.5 dl or 1 cup plain flour
1 tsp baking powder

1. Grease a flan dish.
2. Melt chocolate and butter over hot water.
3. Beat eggs and sugar until fluffy.
4. Add chocolate mixture.
5. Add flour and baking powder and mix well.
6. Put the mixture into the flan dish.
7. Bake for 15 min at Gas 6/7 (425 F/ 200-220 C). You want about 1 inch around the outer edge cooked, and the rest gooey (it keeps on cooking after you take it out of the over).
8. Serve with cream.

Chocolate Raspberry Cake (gluten-free)

CHOCOLATE RASPBERRY CAKE

Sam Schad

This cake is fairly simple to make (with no exotic ingredients) and always popular! It also happens to be gluten-free. Serves 8.

175g plain chocolate
175g caster sugar
5 eggs
1 punnet raspberries
thick cream (I use extra thick double cream)

1. Preheat oven to 180 C.
2. Melt chocolate in a bowl over a pan of simmering water.
3. Line two 18cm tins with a disc of greaseproof paper (put a very little amount of oil in the tin to stick it in)
4. Separate the eggs.
5. Whisk the yolks with the sugar (using an electric whisk).
6. Whisk in the melted chocolate.
7. Whisk in two tablespoons of very hot water to soften the mixture.
8. Whisk the eggs whites. Fold the eggs whites into the mixture.
9. Pour into tins and bake for 18-25 mins.
10. Allow to cool and then chill in fridge.
11. Assemble with thick double cream and raspberries.
12. Decorate with icing sugar or grated chocolate.

GALETTE DES ROIS AU CHOCOLAT

Sam Schad

This cake is traditional for the season of Epiphany in France. It was customary to hide a dried 'bean' inside, which brought luck to the person who found it. Nowadays the 'bean' is often a small trinket or charm, rather like the sixpence my granny used to put in a Christmas pudding.

Serves 6.
Preparation 20 mins; chilling 1 hr; cooking 35-40 mins

2 sheets of puff pastry
1 egg

For the frangipane filling:
100g dark chocolate
100g salted butter
75g soft brown sugar
3 eggs
40g plain flour
100g ground almonds

1. Prepare the frangipane. Melt the chocolate and the butter in a heat-proof bowl for 1 minute in the microwave, then mix in the soft brown sugar, the eggs, the flour, and the ground almonds.
2. On a baking tray covered with greaseproof paper put the first round of puff pastry and spread it with beaten egg. Save the rest of the beaten egg for later.
3. Spread the frangipane over the pastry, leaving a border of 2cm. Put a 'bean' in.
4. Put the second round of pastry on top, pressing it down all round the edge. Chill for 1 hour in the fridge.
5. Preheat the oven to 220 C. With a brush, spread the beaten egg over the pastry, and make a criss-cross pattern with a knife. Bake for 35-40 minutes.

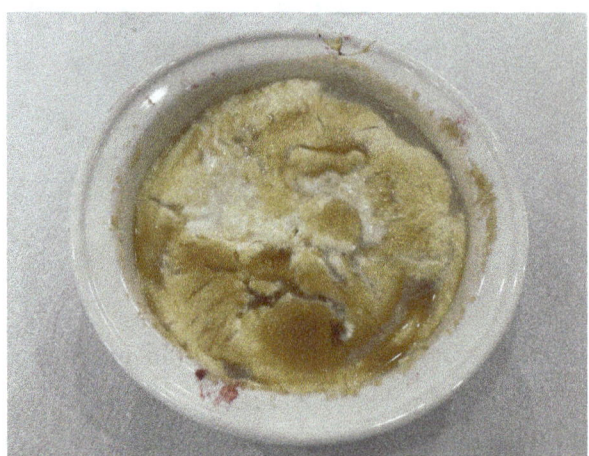

Scottish Trifle

SCOTTISH TRIFLE

Sam Schad

This recipe is from my friend Doreen. She calls it 'raspberry ripple'. I often make it for bring-and-share occasions. I'm not sure why I think it's Scottish, unless it's the raspberries.

This dessert needs to be made the day before.

Serves about 8. You can also double the quantities (you will need a bigger bowl)!

1 packet of trifle sponges or 1 sponge cake cut up
150ml (5 fl. oz.) whipping or double cream
450g plain yoghurt (low fat works well)
450g frozen raspberries
125g (4oz) demerara sugar

1. Line a bowl with the broken sponges and add the frozen raspberries, or layer the sponge and raspberries. If the raspberries are still frozen, leave out of the fridge to defrost for a while.
2. Whip the cream until it reaches the consistency of the yoghurt (not too thick).
3. Mix the cream with the yoghurt, and spread the mixture over the raspberries.
4. Sprinkle the sugar on top.
5. Cover and chill overnight.

Lany Selzer's Cheesecake

LANY SELZER'S CHEESECAKE

Selzer Family

1 lb (450g) butter
2 oz (50g) sugar
1 egg yolk
6 oz (175g) flour
1 teaspoons baking powder
Pinch of salt

Filling:
1 lb (450g) curd cheese
1 tablespoon lemon juice
2 tablespoon corn flour
2 tablespoon cream
4 oz (125g) sugar
1 teaspoon grated orange rind
2 eggs, separated

1. Cream the butter and the sugar; add the egg yolk, then the flour sieved with the baking powder.
2. Mix with a stiff knife and then gather by hand and press into a ball.
3. Chill for 30 minutes and then press into a tart tin. Chill for a further 30 minutes in the fridge.
4. Preheat the oven to 180 C (350 F)
5. Mix all the filling ingredients together except the egg whites.
6. Beat the egg whites stiffly and fold in with a metal spoon.
7. Spoon the filling into the pastry case and bake at 180 C (350 F) for 30 minutes or slightly longer if still too wobbly.

TARTE TATIN

Hugh Series

A French classic, and rightly so.

For the pastry:
125g plain flour
2 tablespoons caster sugar
100g unsalted butter, chilled
Pinch of salt
1 egg yolk
15ml lemon juice (about half the juice of a lemon)

For the filling:
1 kg cooking apples (Bramleys are best. If you use eating apples, reduce the sugar a little)
100g unsalted butter
100g sugar
½ teaspoon cinnamon (optional)

You will need a round pan like a shallow casserole which can go on the hob and then in the oven. Steel or cast iron is good. I use one 26cm across and 6 cm deep, which works well.

1. Start by making the pastry. Mix the sugar and salt into the flour.
2. Rub the chilled butter into the dry mixture until it is like breadcrumbs.
3. Mix the egg yolk and lemon juice and add to the mixture. (You can do all this in a food processor if you prefer).
4. Stir with a knife or spoon until the mixture begins to come together. You may need to add a tiny bit more water (try 1 tablespoon; you shouldn't need more than 2 tablespoons at most).
5. When it starts to clump together, lightly squeeze it with your hands to bring it together into a workable paste, but don't handle it too much or it will start to become warm and a bit greasy.
6. Let it rest in the fridge for about 30 mins.
7. Now heat the oven to 190 C/375 F/gas 5
8. Peel and core the apples. Cut them into segments about 1-2cm thick.

9. Put them in a bowl of water to stop them going brown. Some people add lemon juice to the water to stop the apples going brown, but I have never been convinced that it makes much difference. And anyway, by the time it's all cooked they are a beautiful brown colour in any case.
10. On the hob, melt the second lot of butter in the pan and then pour off about half, reserving it.
11. Add half the sugar to the pan and heat until it starts to caramelise (ie it starts to go brown). Keep tipping the pan to mix the sugar and butter.
12. Add the cinnamon now if you like.
13. Take the pan off the heat and start laying the slices of apple in a pleasing pattern in the bottom of the pan (a spiral like a Catherine wheel looks good), as this is the layer that will on top and visible when you serve it.
14. Continue adding the apple slices, adding the rest of the sugar and melted butter as you go.
15. Take the pastry out of the fridge and roll it out until it is a rough circle just slightly larger than the top of the pan. Lay it over the apples and tuck in the edges around the edge of the pan. No need to worry about making it look neat as this will be at the bottom when served.
16. Cook in the preheated oven for about 45 mins, keeping an eye on it towards the end. The pastry should be brown but not burnt!
17. Take it out of the oven, and let it stand for a few minutes.
18. Wearing oven gloves, put a plate which is slightly larger than the pie upside down over it, and then turn the whole lot upside down so that the plate is now on the table with the upside-down pan sitting on it with the pie inside.
19. Let it stands for a minute or two, and then gently remove the pan. You should be left with a gorgeous brown apple pie, with the pastry layer at the bottom absorbing all the sweet buttery fruity juices.
20. Excellent hot or cold. Serve with cream or ice cream if you wish.

CHOCOLATE FUDGE PUDDING

Talbot-Ponsonby Family

My grandmother's recipe – I don't know where it came from before then. It is very rich and goes well with a good plain ice cream. Serves 4.

3 oz self-raising flour

2 level tbsp cocoa

2 oz margarine

4 oz caster sugar

2 eggs

1-2 tbsp milk

1-2 tsp vanilla essence (optional)

For the sauce:

4 oz soft brown sugar

2 level tbsp cocoa

½ pint hot water

1. Cream together the margarine & sugar.
2. Beat in the eggs (and vanilla) gradually.
3. Mix in the cocoa, then fold in the flour.
4. Mix with enough milk to make a soft consistency. (Alternatively, put all the ingredients in a food processor with a little baking powder and whizz.)
5. Spoon into a baking dish.
6. Mix together cocoa & sugar for sauce in a basin.
7. Stir in hot water.
8. Pour over cake mixture (which will float to the top).
9. Bake for 40 minutes at gas mark 5, 375 F.
10. Serve hot (with ice cream).

ROSE & CARDAMOM BLANCMANGE

Cara Thomas

An easy pudding to make, but use a fine-mesh sieve to avoid any small cardamom seeds in the final pudding

5 leaves gelatine/15g gelatine powder
400ml whole milk
100g sugar, or to taste
2 tsp cardamom pods, lightly crushed
2 tbsp rosewater (mild)
20g shelled unsalted pistachios

1. Soak the gelatine in a small glass of cold water for 5 minutes.
2. Heat the milk together with the sugar and cardamom in a pan to just hot (do not boil), and then turn off the heat.
3. Add rosewater and gelatine and whisk in and leave to cool - approximately 30 minutes.
4. Strain, using a very fine-mesh sieve, into a serving bowl or individual serving bowls and refrigerate to set for a minimum of four hours.
5. Crush the pistachio into small pieces and use to decorate the pudding just before serving.

BISCUITS & CAKES

COCONUT BISCUITS — **EVE BARSHAM**

FAR BRETON PRUNE CAKE — **CLAIRE BROWES**

CHOCOLATE & ORANGE ADVENT CAKE — **MICHÈLE CRAWFORD**

CINNAMON BUNS — **ANNABEL RONALD**

CHRISTMAS CANDIED PECANS — **KATIE RONALD**

LEMON DRIZZLE CAKE — **SOPHIE RONALD**

CHOCOLATE SMARTIES SQUARES — **SAM SCHAD**

GLUTEN-FREE BROWNIES — **SAM SCHAD**

DECADENT CHOCOLATE COOKIES — **SAM SCHAD**

AMARETTI — **HUGH SERIES**

PILGRIM COOKIES — **LUCY SIMMONDS**

FLAPJACKS — **WILL THOMAS**

BAPTIST LEMON CAKE — **DANIEL WALTERS**

BONFIRE NIGHT GINGERBREAD LOAF — **EVA WALTERS**

Coconut Biscuits

COCONUT BISCUITS

Eve Barsham

1 cup of self-raising flour
1 cup of desiccated coconut
1 cup of sugar (preferably brown)
1 cup of porridge oats
Dried fruit, e.g. raisins/sultanas (optional)
3½ oz (100g) margarine from a block
3 tbsp honey or golden syrup

1. Preheat the oven to Gas 3 (170 C).
2. Combine the dry ingredients in a bowl.
3. In a pan gently heat the honey/golden syrup and margarine until melted and mixed and very warm.
4. Pour the liquid over the dry ingredients and mix well.
5. Press the mixture onto a greased baking tray (I used a 20cm square tin) and cook on the top shelf of the oven for 15-18 minutes, until a light brown colour. Turn the tin around halfway.
6. Remove from the oven and after a few minutes score with a knife into individual pieces.
7. Allow to cool completely, then prise the pieces out with a knife. When cold store in an airtight tin.

Far Breton Prune Cake

FAR BRETON PRUNE CAKE

Claire Browes

This is another recipe from the French side of the family and is a traditional pudding from Brittany. You can buy it by the slice in bakeries or on markets, but my grandma, and Mum, both made them, and I make them at home too.

It is served cold and has a sort of custard-jelly like texture that not everyone is sure about! You can make it without the prunes and have a 'Far Breton Nature'.

200g plain flour
50g caster sugar
750ml milk
4 eggs
20-25 prunes
Rum (to taste, optional)
Vanilla Essence

1. Mix together the flour and eggs one-by-one with a whisk.
2. Add the sugar and then the milk slowly.
3. Add the rum (if using), milk and the vanilla essence.
4. Pour into a shallow over-proof dish and leave to stand for 1hr.
5. Preheat the oven to 200C.
6. Add prunes into the dish evenly.
7. Bake for 45 mins. The top can get quite dark – that is normal!
8. Cool before serving and keep in the fridge.

Chocolate & Orange Advent Cake

The decoration represents a pie chart of the liturgical seasons. You can use:
Green for ordinary time
Yellow/White for Christmas and Easter
Red for Pentecost

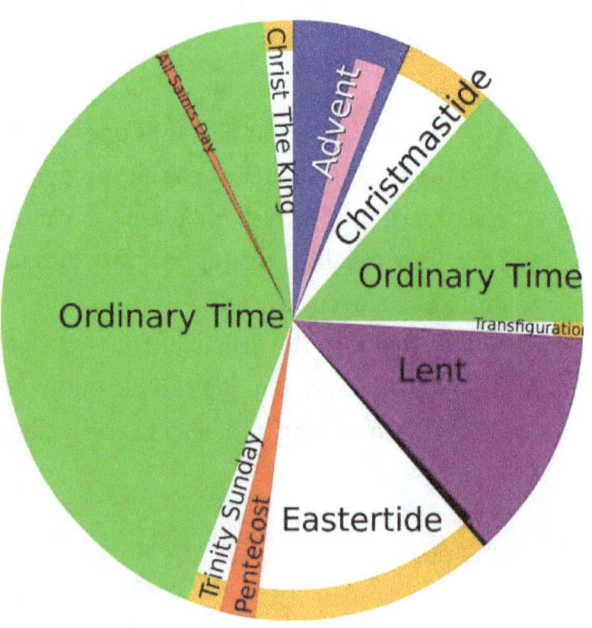

CHOCOLATE & ORANGE ADVENT CAKE

Michèle Crawford

The basic cake is from Nigella Lawson.
The décor is pure Michèle! Serves about 8.

2 small or 1 large thin-skinned orange, approx. 375g total weight
6 eggs
1 heaped tsp baking powder
½ tsp bicarbonate of soda
200g ground almonds
250g caster sugar
50g cocoa
coloured icing (red, yellow, green, blue and white)

You will need a 20-23cm springform tin.

1. Put the whole orange or oranges in a pan with some cold water, bring to the boil and cook for 2 hours or until soft.
2. Drain and, when cool, cut the oranges in half and remove any big pips.
3. Then pulp everything – pith, peel and all – in a food processor, or see below if you're proceeding by hand. You can do all this the day before.
4. Once the fruit is cold, or near cold, preheat the oven to gas mark 4/180°C.
5. Butter and line a 20cm springform tin.
6. Add the eggs, baking powder, bicarbonate of soda, almonds, sugar and cocoa to the orange in the food processor. Run the motor until you have a cohesive cake mixture, but still slightly knobbly with the flecks of puréed orange. Or you could chop the fruit finely by hand, and with a wooden spoon beat the eggs one by one into the sugar, alternating with spoons of mixed ground almonds and cocoa, then the oranges.
7. Pour and scrape into the cake tin and bake for an hour, by which time a cake tester should come out pretty well clean.
8. Check after 45 minutes because you may have to cover with foil to prevent the cake burning before it is cooked through.
9. Leave the cake to get cool in the tin, on a cooling rack. When the cake is cold you can take it out of the tin and decorate as in the picture opposite.

92 - ST. MARGARET'S CHURCH

CINNAMON BUNS

Annabel Ronald

For the dough:
200g full fat milk
2 medium eggs
500g strong white bread flour
25g fresh yeast
50g caster sugar
10g salt
200g unsalted butter

For the filling:
150g unsalted butter
250g soft brown sugar
2tsp cinnamon

For the egg glaze:
1 egg
2 tbsp full fat milk
For the sugar glaze:
100g caster sugar
100g water

1. Start by making the dough. Put the milk and eggs into the bowl of a food mixer, then add the flour.
2. Break in the yeast to one side of the bowl, then add the salt and sugar and butter to the other side.
3. Mix on a slow speed for 4 minutes, then increase the speed to medium and mix for a further 10-12 minutes until the dough comes away cleanly from the side of the bowl.
4. Form the dough into a ball and pop into a clean floured bowl. Cover and leave for around 45 minutes or until double in size.
5. Lightly flour a work surface and roll the dough into a rectangle roughly the size of an A3 sheet of paper.

6. For the filling, beat the butter and sugar together until pale and stir in the cinnamon. Spread the filling over the top of the dough.
7. With the long side facing you, fold in half lengthways to enclose the filling and slice it widthways into 24 strips each roughly 3.5cm across. Next, use a sharp knife to cut twice down the length of each strip to make three strands. Plait the three strands together and repeat to make 24 individual plaits.
8. Take each plait and roll it up along its length to create a knot. Grease a 12-cup muffin tray and pop the knots onto the tray. Cover and allow to prove for 1 hour.
9. Aim to have your wood-fired oven at around 200 C with little to no flame. Brush the knots with the egg glaze and pop into the oven to bake for 15-20 minutes until golden.
10. Meanwhile make the sugar glaze. Put the sugar and water in a pan and bring to the boil, turn down to a simmer until you have a light syrup.
11. Brush the baked knots with the syrup while still hot and leave to cool before devouring.

CHRISTMAS CANDIED PECANS

Katie Ronald

You can also add some ground cloves
and nutmeg, but it isn't necessary!

1 lb (450g) pecan halves
1 large egg white
1 tbsp water
½ tsp vanilla extract
1 cup granulated sugar
1 tsp cinnamon
½ tsp salt

1. Preheat the oven to 120 C. Line an 18x13 inch (45x33 cm) baking sheet with parchment paper.
2. Whisk the wet ingredients: in a large mixing bowl, vigorously whisk the egg white with the water and vanilla until very frothy.
3. Whisk the dry ingredients: in a separate small mixing bowl, whisk together the sugar, cinnamon and salt.
4. Toss the pecans with the wet ingredients: add the pecans to the egg white mixture and toss until evenly coated.
5. Toss the pecans with the sugar mixture: pour the sugar mixture over the pecans and toss until evenly coated.
6. Spread the coated nuts onto a baking sheet: pour the coated pecans over a parchment paper-lined baking sheet and spread into an even layer.
7. Bake until crisp: bake in a pre-heated oven for 1 hour, stirring every 15 minutes. Allow to cool.

Lemon Drizzle Cake

LEMON DRIZZLE CAKE

Sophie Ronald

This is a Mary Berry recipe. I make the recipe using half quantities, in a smaller tin (18 x 28cm or 7 x 11 in), and cook it for less time (20-25 minutes), as I find the drizzle sinks into a shallower cake more effectively. I also pierce the warm cake with a skewer or fondue fork to help the drizzle penetrate the sponge.
Makes 16 slices.

For the cake:
225g (8oz) butter (room temperature) or spread (at least 70% fat), plus extra for greasing
225g (8oz) caster sugar
275g (9.5oz) self-raising flour
1 tsp baking powder
4 large eggs
4 tbsp milk
Grated zest of 1 lemon
For the glaze:
Juice of 2 lemons
175g (6oz) granulated sugar

1. Preheat the oven to 180 C (fan 160 C/350 F/ Gas 4). Grease a traybake tin measuring 30 x 23cm (12 x 9 in) and 4cm (1.5 in) deep, and line the base with baking parchment.
2. Place the butter, sugar, flour, baking powder, eggs, milk, and lemon zest in a bowl. Beat with an electric mixer for 1-2 minutes, or with a wooden spoon for a little longer, until smooth.
3. Turn the mixture into the lined tin and spread evenly. Line a spatula to smooth and scrape up all the mixture around the sides of the bowl.
4. Bake in the preheated oven for 35-40 minutes, or until risen and springy to the touch.
5. Run a knife around the edge of the traybake to loosen it from the tin, then transfer to a wire rack.
6. Make the glaze: mix the lemon juice with the sugar and spoon over the warm cake. Leave to cool, then cut into 16 rectangular slices.

Chocolate Smarties Squares

CHOCOLATE SMARTIES SQUARES

Sam Schad

Makes 24 small squares.

For the Cake:
4oz butter
4oz caster sugar
2 eggs
1 oz cocoa powder
3 oz self-raising flour
1 tbsp milk

For the Icing:
4oz butter
1.5 oz cocoa powder
6.5 oz icing sugar
1 tbsp milk
smarties to decorate

1. Preheat oven to 190 C. Line a 7x11" (18x25cm) tin with greaseproof paper.
2. Cream butter and sugar till light and fluffy.
3. Add eggs one at a time, mixing in each one.
4. Add cocoa and flour and mix in.
5. Add milk and mix in. Put mixture in tin. Bake for about 20 minutes until springy.
6. Icing: cream butter with half cocoa-and-icing-sugar.
7. Add the rest of the cocoa-and-icing-sugar, together with the milk. Mix.
8. Spread icing on cake. Decorated with smarties. Cut into squares.

Gluten-free Brownies

GLUTEN-FREE BROWNIES

Sam Schad

This recipe is from the Co-op magazine. It was sent in by Kelsey Tobolik. Because they are made without flour they are quite squidgy and not dry like some gluten-free cakes. Makes about 20.

150g dark chocolate
190g unsalted butter
150g light soft brown sugar
3 eggs
1 tbsp cocoa powder
1 tsp baking powder
150g white chocolate, finely chopped

1. Preheat the oven to 170 C (Gas 4).
2. Grease and line a square tin (about 20cm) with greaseproof paper.
3. Add the dark chocolate and butter to a large bowl and melt over a pan of simmering water.
4. Take off the heat, stir in the sugar, then cool for 10 minutes.
5. Beat the eggs, then gradually whisk them in.
6. Stir in the cocoa and baking powder, and stir in the white chocolate.
7. Pour the mixture into the prepared tin and bake in the oven for about 50 minutes until risen and crispy on the top but still gooey in the middle. (In fact I bake for about 25 minutes).
8. Leave to cool completely in the tin before cutting into squares.

Decadent Chocolate Cookies

DECADENT CHOCOLATE COOKIES

Sam Schad

This recipe is from my friend Rebecca. She calls it 'more chocolate than cookies'. I often make them
to fuel the choir before evensong, but I fear they may not be the best thing for singing.
Makes 12-20 (depending on size).

175g plain chocolate, chopped
100g unsalted butter, cut into pieces
2 eggs
100g sugar
40g soft brown sugar
40g plain flour
40g cocoa powder
1tsp baking powder
¼ tsp salt
500g (approx.) mixed chocolate, chopped into small pieces

1. Preheat the oven to 170 C/325 F.
2. Grease two large baking sheets, or cover with greaseproof paper.
3. In a medium saucepan, over a low heat, melt the chocolate (100g) and butter, stirring frequently until smooth. Remove from heat to cool slightly.
4. Beat the eggs and sugars until thick and pale, 2-3 minutes.
5. Gradually pour in the melted chocolate, beating until well blended.
6. Beat in the flour, cocoa powder, and salt until just blended. Stir in the mixed chocolate pieces (500g).
7. Drop heaped tablespoonfuls of dough on the baking sheets at least 10cm apart, flattening the dough slightly. You will only get 4-6 cookies on each sheet.
8. Bake for 10-12 minutes or until the tops are shiny and cracked. Do not overbake or they will crack when removed from the sheet.
9. Remove the baking sheets to a wire rack to cool until the cookies are firm, but not too crisp, THEN transfer each cookie to the wire rack to cool completely.
10. Continue to bake in batches.

11. Store the cookies in an airtight container (if there are any left).

AMARETTI

Hugh Series

Handy for times when you need to take some sweet delicacies for a party after Evensong (or to cheer up the choir in between the rehearsal and the service).
Makes about 30 (you need 2 large oven trays)

2 eggs, whites only (80g/3oz)

170g/6oz caster sugar

170g/6oz ground almonds

15ml amaretto liqueur (don't be tempted to add more liquid, but you can try substituting 5ml almond extract)

1. Preheat the oven to 170C/325F/Gas 3.
2. In a large bowl beat the egg whites until firm.
3. Fold the sugar and the almonds gently into it.
4. Add the amaretto liquor/almond extract and fold in gently until you have a smooth paste which should be fairly stiff.
5. Place some baking paper (or a reusable silicone baking mat) on a baking tray and lightly brush with butter (you don't need the butter for a silicone mat).
6. Using a teaspoon place small heaps of the mixture approximately 2cm/¾in apart, as they will expand whilst cooking. They look best if you leave them rough like little mountains, but if your mixture is a bit softer and they spread into flatter hillocks, then they will still taste just as good.
7. Bake for approximately 20-25 minutes until golden brown.
8. Leave to cool slightly then dust thickly with icing sugar just before serving.

Pilgrim Cookies

PILGRIM COOKIES

Lucy Simmonds

Here's the recipe that I used for last year's pilgrimage chocolate chip cookies.
Sadly it's not Michèle's legendary recipe which really was the best,
but I didn't hear any complaints about these ones from the Pilgrims!

140g butter, softened in the microwave
75g golden caster sugar
75g light brown muscovado sugar
1 egg
1-2 tsp vanilla extract
175g plain flour
1 tsp baking powder
Pinch of salt (optional)
200g chocolate of your choice, chopped into chunks

1. Cream the butter and sugar.
2. Add vanilla extract and the egg and mix.
3. Stir in the flour, baking powder and salt, followed by the chocolate.
4. Roll the dough into balls and put onto a baking tray lined with baking parchment.
5. Put the tray in the fridge for at least an hour (overnight is even better).
6. Take the tray straight from the fridge and bake at 160 degrees fan until the edges are just firm but the middle is still soft.

FLAPJACKS

Will Thomas

250g jumbo porridge oats
150g butter, plus extra for the tin
200g light brown sugar
1 tbsp golden syrup

1. Heat the oven to 200oC/180oC fan/gas 6.
2. Put the oats, butter, sugar and golden syrup in a food processor and pulse until mixed.
3. Grease a 20 x 20cm baking tin and add the mixture.
4. Press into the corners with your fingers so the mixture is flat and score into fingers.
5. Bake for around 15 mins until golden brown.
6. Leave to cool completely before removing from the tin.

BAPTIST LEMON CAKE

Daniel Walters

Daniel found this recipe in a Baptist daily Bible readings pamphlet
when he was little and made his mum make it with him.
It's become a family favourite and his mum still has the original recipe.

1 small pot of natural yoghurt
1 yoghurt pot of oil
2 yoghurt pots of caster sugar
3 yoghurt pots of self raising flour
3 well beaten eggs
Lemon icing, e.g. lemon glace icing or lemon butter-cream icing.

1. Mix all the ingredients together very well.
2. Pour the mixture into a lightly greased tin.
3. Bake for 1 hour at 180C.
4. When the cake has cooked and cooled, cover with lemon icing.

BONFIRE NIGHT GINGERBREAD LOAF

Eva Walters

125g butter
125g golden syrup
150g dark treacle
125g brown sugar
275g plain flour
Half tsp salt
2 tsp ground ginger
1 tsp cinnamon
1 level tsp bicarbonate of soda
1 beaten egg
225ml sour milk or milk with a squirt of lemon

1. Grease tin & line with grease proof paper
2. Melt butter, syrup, treacle & sugar gently in a pan. Allow to cool.
3. Sieve together flour, ginger, salt, cinnamon and bicarbonate of soda.
4. Pour contents of pan into flour.
5. Beat in egg and milk.
6. Pour into tin.
7. Bake in a moderate oven at 160C for about an hour, checking after 50mins.
8. Turn out of tin onto wire rack and cool.